D1530967

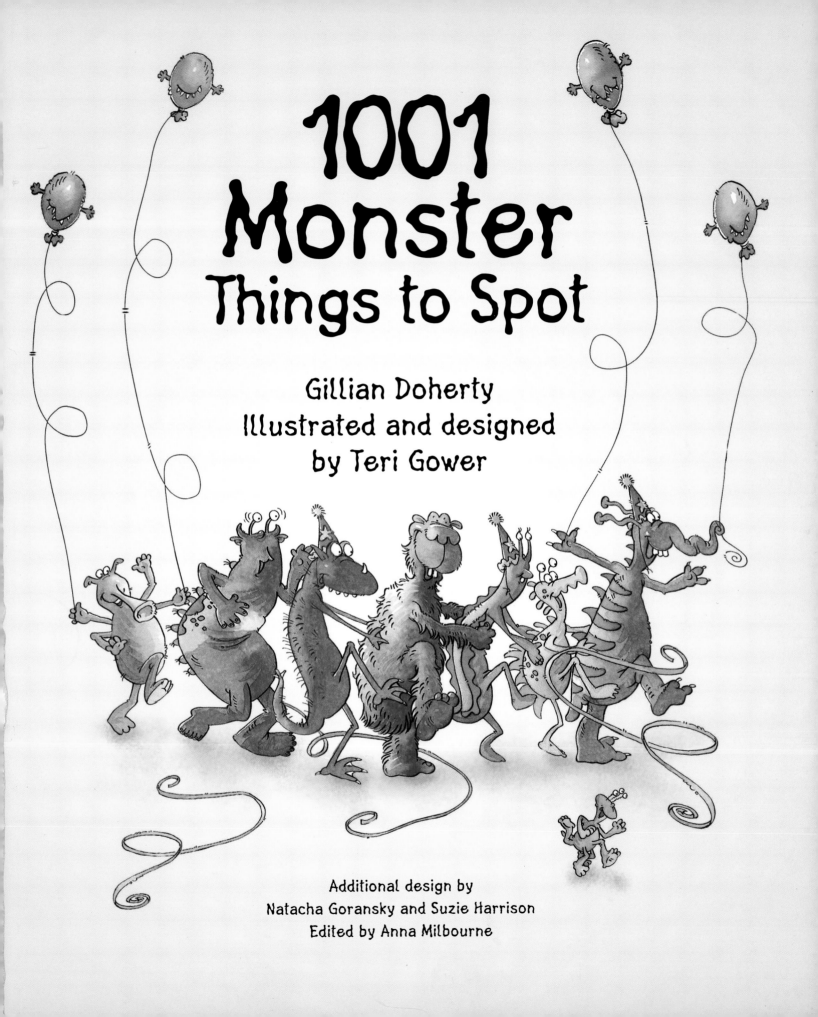

1001 Monster Things to Spot

Gillian Doherty

Illustrated and designed
by Teri Gower

Additional design by
Natacha Goransky and Suzie Harrison
Edited by Anna Milbourne

Contents

Things to Spot

Monsters come in all shapes and sizes. Most of them are very friendly, as you'll find out when you explore their monster world.

In each scene there are all kinds of monstrosities for you to find and count. There are 1001 things to spot altogether.

Monster Party

5 clodhoppers   6 trombugles   8 wowows   9 party hats   1 monstrous cake   8 monster poppers   10 monster balloons   9 boogaloos   6 striped presents   4 humdingers

26   27

Each little picture shows you what to look for in the big picture.

The number tells you how many of that thing you need to find.

Billy is crazy about monsters and when he grows up he wants to be a monsterologist. Can you find him tracking monsters in every scene?

Bedroom Monsters

7 clambermanders

5 astro monsters

7 slumber busters

6 pingles

8 bubble beasts

5 pocket trolls

10 sock eaters

3 toy rockets

6 doodle monsters

9 scufflebumps

Midnight Feast

7 nibblers

10 scoffits

9 monster muffins

8 gobblitos

4 bottles of monsterade

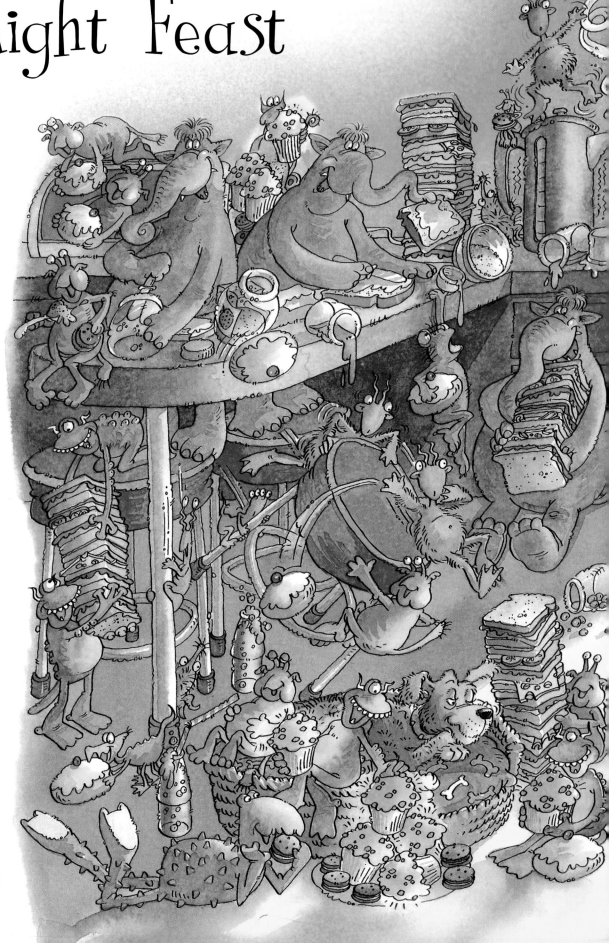

3 bellyphants

10 sticky buns

9 pot-bellied flimbos

6 chomps

5 towering sandwiches

Monster Nursery

10 roaring rattles 5 toddling sproggles 9 toy monsters 7 fuzzy grizzles 6 mollycoddles

2 monster mobiles

10 jigsaw pieces

3 naughty ninkles

5 diddums with messy bibs

7 monster storybooks

9

Freaky Market

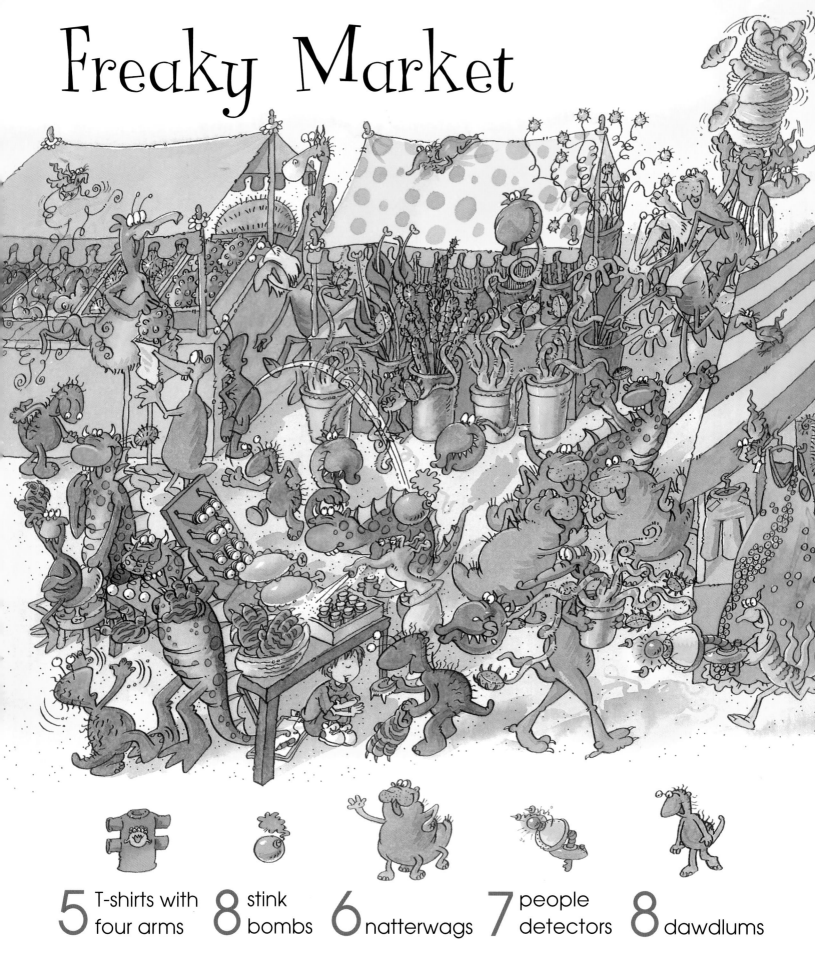

5 T-shirts with four arms   8 stink bombs   6 natterwags   7 people detectors   8 dawdlums

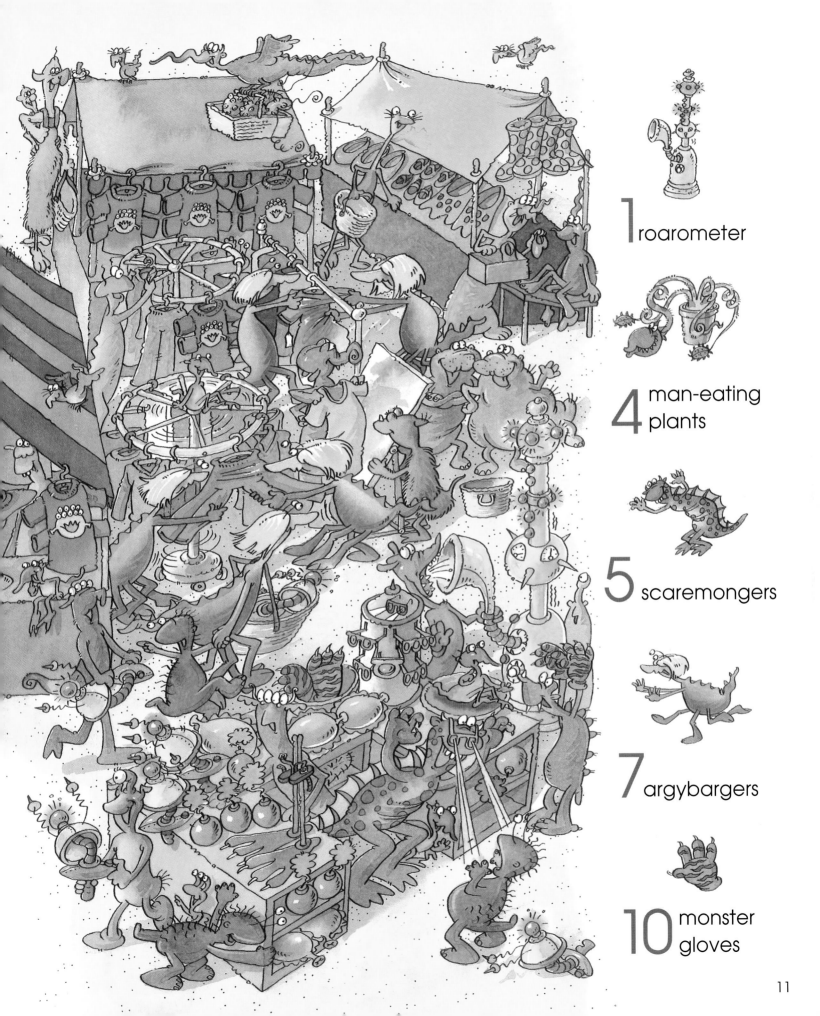

1 roarometer

4 man-eating plants

5 scaremongers

7 argybargers

10 monster gloves

Monster Park

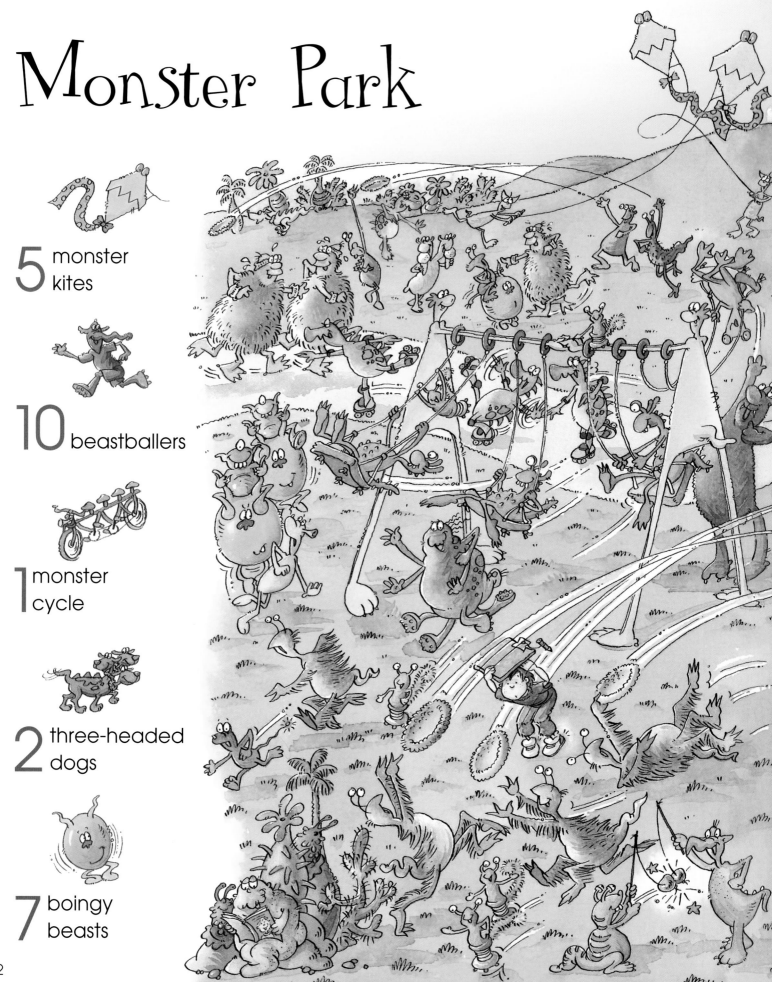

5 monster kites

10 beastballers

1 monster cycle

2 three-headed dogs

7 boingy beasts

10 fuzzy frisbees 9 hopadoos 6 zoobers skating 3 quimbles on swings 5 hurlyburbles

Beastly School

4 misfangles 6 yellow munchboxes 8 swotty blots 9 school ties 7 one-eyed gumps

5 polkadot backpacks

7 scamps

9 paper planes

10 pen porters

6 quagvarks

Creepy Camp

7 snugglebugs

9 giant spiders

8 owligators

1 campfire

10 spooky lanterns

6 hairy howlers

3 growling guitars

10 monstrous shadows

9 buzzwings

8 shufflesnaps

Beach Beasts

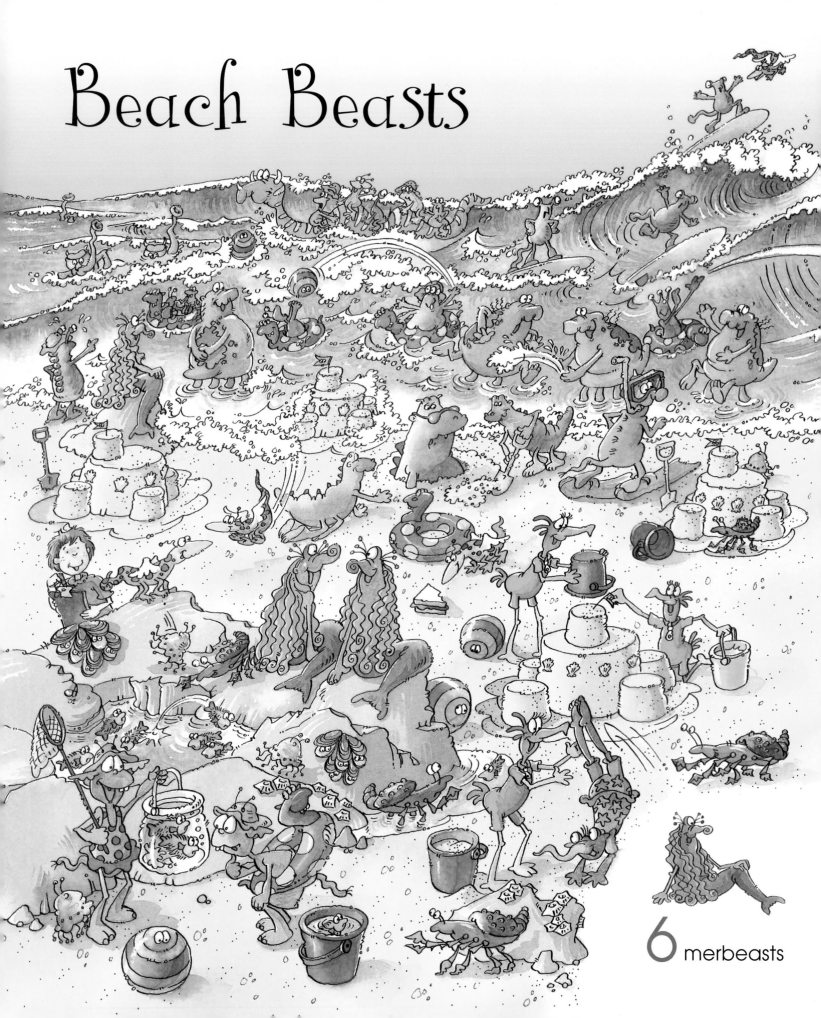

6 merbeasts

10 rubber rings

6 giant sandcastles

9 craggles

8 beach balls

8 bobsurfers

10 furry fish

7 bloops

9 wingles

2 sea squibbles

Carnival Parade

1 huffalump

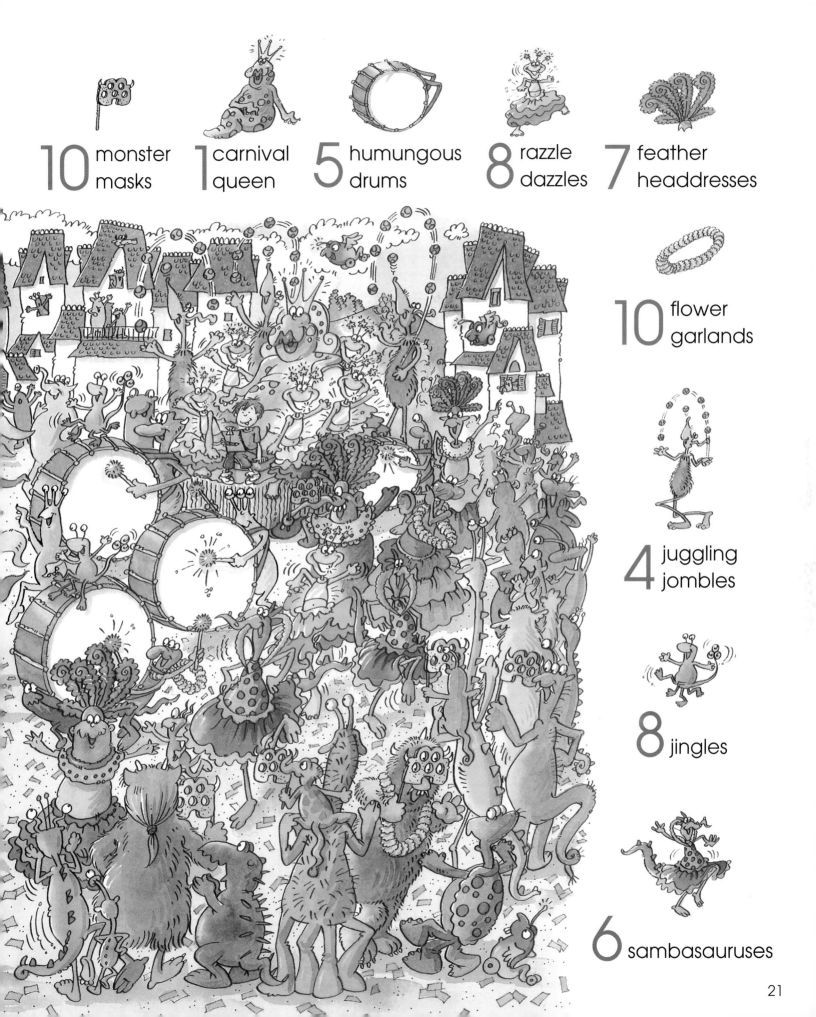

10 monster masks

1 carnival queen

5 humungous drums

8 razzle dazzles

7 feather headdresses

10 flower garlands

4 juggling jombles

8 jingles

6 sambasauruses

Monster Hospital

4 clomps with broken tails

10 freaky flowers

9 sick snooks

7 wiggly stethoscopes

8 monstrous x-rays

10 pootles 4 octodoctors 8 noddle nurses 5 wuffles with lumpitis 9 furry crutches

Beauty Salon

8 powder puffs

5 beasticians

9 yellow rollers

10 bottles of claw varnish

7 ugly mugglies

9 pink bows **4** monster furdryers **10** snippets **7** bigwigs **8** splendiferoos

Monster Party

5 clodhoppers   6 trombugles   8 wowows   9 party hats   1 monstrous cake

8 monster poppers   10 monster balloons   9 boogaloos   6 striped presents   4 humdingers

Snow Monsters

10 huge footprints

5 yetis

8 skidoobles

9 frostbiters

3 ice giants

10 snowballs

6 snow buggies

7 snozzlebird ski lifts

4 snow monsters

9 pairs of earmuffs

Monster Gallery

Not all monsters are big and bold. Some are shy and tricky to spot. Billy's pictures of some of these bashful beasts are on show at the monster gallery. Can you find them throughout the book?

7 hushabillies

10 shadow huggers

6 phobies

8 skulks

9 heebie jeebies

6 dweebles

8 bashflubbers

10 jitterbugs

9 grimples

5 blushums

9 wheedles

7 peekaboos

8 quivers

31

Answers

Did you find all the shy monsters from the monster gallery? Here's where they are:

10 shadow huggers
Bedroom Monsters
(pages 4–5)

6 phobies
Freaky Market
(pages 10–11)

8 skulks
Midnight Feast
(pages 6–7)

7 hushabillies
Monster Hospital
(pages 22–23)

9 heebie jeebies
Creepy Camp
(pages 16–17)

6 dweebles
Beastly School
(pages 14–15)

8 bashflubbers
Monster Park
(pages 12–13)

10 jitterbugs
Monster Party
(pages 26–27)

9 grimples
Snow Monsters
(pages 28–29)

5 blushums
Beauty Salon
(pages 24–25)

9 wheedles
Carnival Parade
(pages 20–21)

7 peekaboos
Monster Nursery
(pages 8–9)

8 quivers
Beach Beasts
(pages 18–19)

First published in 2008 by Usborne Publishing Ltd.,
Usborne House, 83-85 Saffron Hill, London EC1N 8RT, England. www.usborne.co.uk
First published in America in 2008. UE. Printed in China.